craft **workshop**

appliqué

craft **workshop**

appliqué

Petra Boase

photography by Polly Wreford

southwater

This edition is published by Southwater

Southwater is an imprint of Anness Publishing Ltd
Hermes House, 88–89 Blackfriars Road, London SE1 8HA
tel. 020 7401 2077; fax 020 7633 9499
www.southwaterbooks.com; info@anness.com

© Anness Publishing Ltd 1997, 2003

This edition distributed in the UK by The Manning
Partnership Ltd, 6 The Old Dairy,
Melcombe Road, Bath BA2 3LR;
tel. 01225 478 444; fax 01225 478 440;
sales@manning-partnership.co.uk

This edition distributed in the USA and Canada by National
Book Network, 4720 Boston Way, Lanham, MD 20706;
tel. 301 459 3366; fax 301 459 1705; www.nbnbooks.com

This edition distributed in Australia by Pan Macmillan
Australia, Level 18, St Martins Tower,
31 Market St, Sydney, NSW 2000;
tel. 1300 135 113; fax 1300 135 103;
customer.service@macmillan.com.au

This edition distributed in New Zealand by The Five Mile
Press (NZ) Ltd, PO Box 33–1071 Takapuna, Unit
11/101–111 Diana Drive, Glenfield, Auckland 10;
tel. (09) 444 4144; fax (09) 444 4518;
fivemilenz@clear.net.nz

Previously published as *New Crafts: Appliqué*

PUBLISHER: JOANNA LORENZ
SENIOR EDITOR: LINDSAY PORTER
DESIGNER: LILIAN LINDBLOM
STEP PHOTOGRAPHER: MARK WOOD
STYLIST: LEEANN MACKENZIE
ILLUSTRATORS: MADELEINE DAVID AND
VANA HAGGERTY

PICTURE CREDITS
Thanks to e.t. archive for the photographs on pages 8, 9, 10
and 11.

10 9 8 7 6 5 4 3 2 1

PICTURE CREDITS
The author and publishers would like to thank the following for additional photography: by courtesy of the board of trustees of the Victoria and Albert Museum, pp 8 and 9;
Patrick Gorman, p 10 and Joseph Ortenzi, p 17

CONTENTS

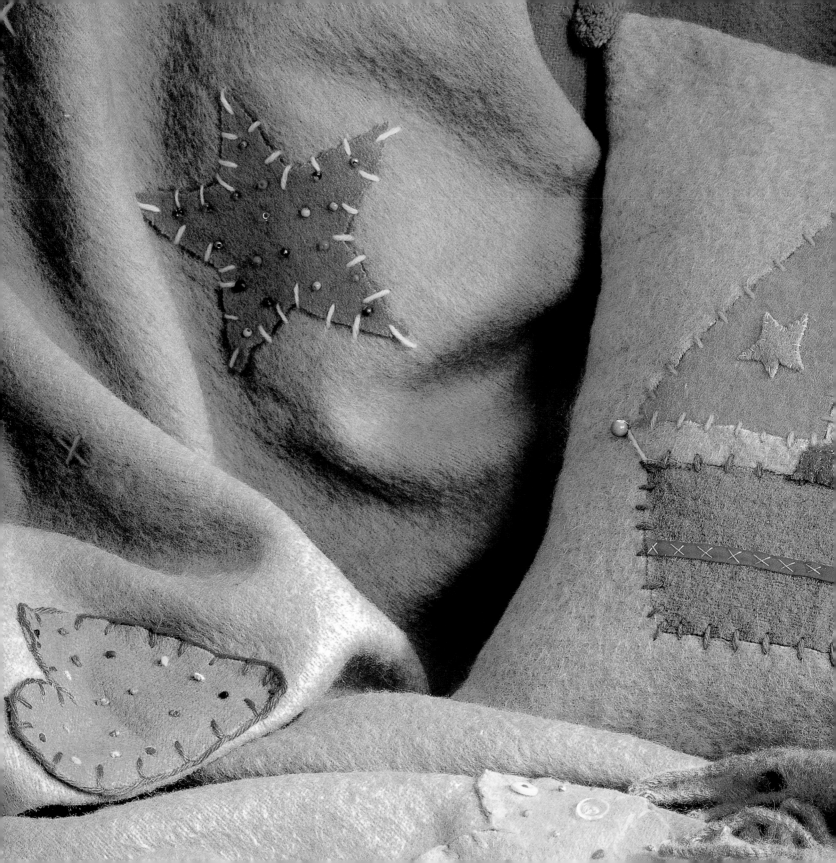

INTRODUCTION

PPLIQUÉ IS A VERY VERSATILE METHOD OF APPLYING AND SECURING PIECES OF FABRIC ON TO A BACKGROUND WHICH IS THEN ENRICHED BY DECORATIVE STITCHES. APPLIQUÉ HAS BEEN PRACTISED ALL OVER THE WORLD FOR CENTURIES, WITH MANY DIFFERENT STYLES AND TECHNIQUES DEVELOPING. THERE ARE NO LIMITATIONS TO THE METHODS OF APPLIQUÉ: IT CAN BE BOLD AND COLOURFUL, PICTORIAL OR ABSTRACT AND BOTH SIMPLE AND COMPLEX DESIGNS CAN BE CREATED. THE 25 DIVERSE AND EXCITING PROJECTS IN THIS BOOK ARE EXAMPLES OF DIFFERENT METHODS OF APPLIQUÉ USING AN ASSORTMENT OF INTERESTING FABRICS AND DECORATIVE TRIMMINGS AND STITCHES TO CREATE INSPIRING ITEMS FOR YOU TO MAKE.

Left: Simple shapes in ice-cream colours are used to great effect in these appliqué designs, illustrating that strikingly contemporary pieces can be created from an age-old technique.

HISTORY OF APPLIQUÉ

APPLIQUÉ HAS BEEN PRACTISED FOR CENTURIES BY MOST CULTURES THROUGHOUT THE WORLD. ITS ORIGINS WERE INITIALLY PRACTICAL: SCRAPS OF CLOTH COULD BE RE-USED BY SEWING THEM TO BACKGROUND FABRICS, THUS PROLONGING THE LIFE OF CLOTHING AND MATERIALS THAT MAY HAVE BEEN SCARCE. IT IS INTERESTING TO TRACE HOW THESE CONCERNS INSPIRED A MEANS OF CREATIVE EXPRESSION; THE FABRICS COULD BE CUT INTO ATTRACTIVE SHAPES AND EMBELLISHED WITH STITCHING. AS DIFFERENT TECHNIQUES DEVELOPED INDEPENDENTLY THROUGHOUT THE WORLD, VARYING STYLES EMERGED.

Although appliqué developed very simply as a method of repairing worn items of clothing, examples have been found dating back as far as 980 BC when animal hides were used by the ancient Egyptians to embellish funeral tents.

During the Middle Ages, appliqué became a very fashionable and functional method of working for needleworkers: because of its relatively low cost, it became a very strong substitute for the more costly and time-consuming solid embroidery. Fabrics were applied to items as diverse as household furnishings, heraldic flags and costumes. Appliqué was especially popular on ecclesiastical robes and altar frontals. In these instances linen shapes were cut out and applied on to a velvet or silk background with an edging of cord or silk strands. The appliquéd shapes would then be embellished with rich gold stitching.

During the Renaissance, appliqué became a lavish form of embellishment on furnishings and hangings throughout the palaces and castles of the upper classes and royalty. As well as being exquisitely executed and beautifully decorated, many of the appliquéd hangings were hung and draped around the home for warmth, especially in doorways and around four-poster beds to shut out draughts.

In peasant cultures, the appliqué tradition was equally strong: precious remnants of more costly fabrics such as silk would be cut into shapes and appliquéd on to damaged parts of clothing or applied to domestic articles. This grew from economic necessity, but it also created many sophisticated results. Thus appliqué became strongly associated with folk art, and evidence of the technique appears in most cultures throughout the world. In Hungary, leather appliqué became very popular among peasant societies and was very much a status symbol because of the expense involved.

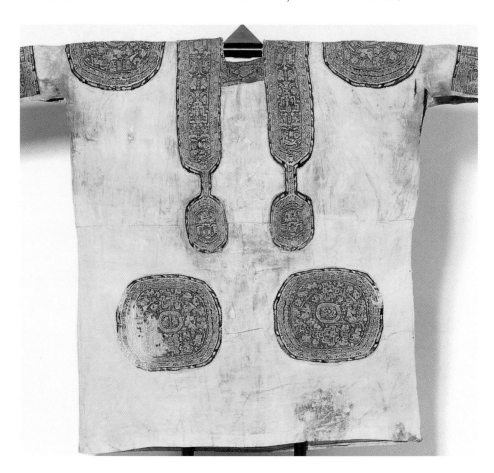

Above: Appliqué examples have been found dating back centuries, and practical motives, such as repairing worn cloth, soon gave way to decorative effects. This leather tunic dates from 6-7th century AD. The appliqué inserts are made from woven tapestry.

Throughout the United States, appliqué developed independently through quilt designs. Patterns were handed down from generation to generation and were often based on natural imagery such as birds, baskets, fruit, bouquets of flowers and garlands. Economy made the quilt popular throughout America as each scrap of fabric left over from cutting clothing was saved, and quilts were an essential part of the home for practical reasons because of the austere winters. Some quilts had so much work put into them that they were often kept for privileged guests or for display in the home.

Many of the techniques that inspire contemporary work draw on the intricate and unusual methods practised throughout South East Asia and India. In India, appliqué was commonly used to make religious hangings for festivals and ceremonies. The fabrics chosen would often depend on the importance of the event. The images portrayed throughout the designs were often drawn from mythology and were very spiritually symbolic. In South East Asia, intricate maze patterns were created using a cut-work method. The designs were highly intricate and were used in the decoration of clothing and hangings. In many tribes the skill is still a very central part of women's work. The 20th century brought exciting and innovative design movements. Today, appliqué is rich and varied in style and is used for many different applications. Many of the methods used are drawn from traditional techniques practised through history all over the world. Machine-stitching has become a very popular method of applying and embellishing appliqué shapes and there are now many forms of fabric bondings and adhesives on the market to aid faster methods of appliqué. Appliqué is often seen as the fabric equivalent to

paper collage and should be executed in a similarly spontaneous way. Be as expressive as you wish with your choice of fabrics and embellishments, and don't let complicated techniques restrict the flow and imagination of your designs.

Above: A beautiful example of a decorative panel dating from 19th century Persia. Brightly coloured woollen cloth pieces were applied to a main background fabric and embellished with decorative embroidery stitches, including chain stitch. This exquisite example of the needleworker's art combines many of the most appealing aspects of appliqué.

GALLERY

DESIGNERS TODAY ARE USING APPLIQUÉ TO CREATE AN OUTSTANDING RANGE OF OBJECTS AND EFFECTS. THE PIECES ON THE FOLLOWING PAGES START WITH THE SAME BASIC TECHNIQUE BUT THE RESULTS ARE AS DIVERSE AS THEIR CREATORS. THE FOLLOWING EXAMPLES USE MATERIALS FROM PAPER TO PLASTIC AND ALL MANNER OF NATURAL FABRICS. LET THEM BE A STARTING POINT FOR YOUR OWN PERSONAL CREATIONS.

Right: NOUGHTS AND CROSSES
This embroidered wall hanging is made in nine sections using a combination of hand- and machine-stitching to appliqué silk, cotton, chiffon and velvet on to a background fabric.
CHARLOTTE HODGE

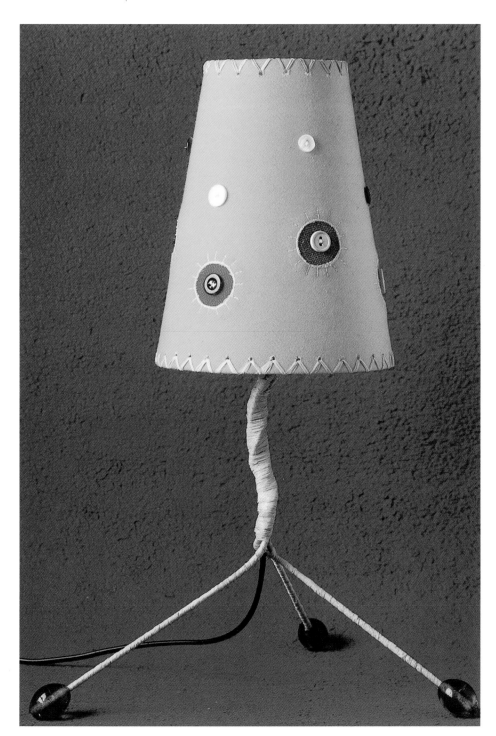

Left: SPOT LAMPSHADE
A fabric-covered shade is embellished with buttons and bright circles of colour using the cut-work technique. The appliqué shapes are sewn behind the background fabric which is then cut away to reveal the new colours beneath.
HELEN RAWLINSON

Above: SHOWER CURTAIN
Brightly coloured PVC fabric and bold designs are used to great effect in this eye-catching design.
ANNE DELAUNEY

Far right and right: PAPER APPLIQUÉ HANGING AND DETAIL
The ingenious combination of materials and subtle tones makes this piece very striking. Hand-made paper squares are stitched on to a background fabric. Small squares of hand-painted muslin form the central motif.
CHRISTINE SMITH

Left: WALL HANGING
The artist uses photographic images transferred on to fabric, which are then appliquéd on to a background fabric.
NATASHA KERR

Opposite: HAT AND PURSE
These pieces were made by first hand-knitting the basic shapes and felting them by washing in warm soapy water. When dry the elements are sewn together, with additional felted knitting and commercial felt appliquéd on top. The resulting richly textured fabric is wonderfully tactile.
TERESA SEARLE

Right: SHADOW-APPLIQUÉ WAISTCOAT
Natural linen forms the basis of this waistcoat, made special by the appliqué designs on the pockets. The pattern pieces were cut from scraps of coloured silk, machine-stitched in place, then covered with a layer of organza.
LOUISE BROWNLOW

Right: CHILD'S CARDIGAN
Felt patchwork pieces in harlequin colours are decorated with simple felt shapes held in place with contrasting coloured threads. Blanket stitch finishes off the cuffs and hems.
KATIE MAWSON

Above: WALL HANGING
Architectural shapes are used in an almost abstract manner in this appliquéd and machine-embroidered hanging.
CHARLOTTE HODGE

Left: HAT AND SCARF
This matching hat and scarf set for a child is a perfect example of how simple yet strong embellishments can transform an object. Rich textures, bold colours and stitches all combine to make an appealing and original design.
KATIE MAWSON

Above: SPONGE BAG
The perfect accessory for the designer's shower curtain, the basic shape was made using a patchwork technique, then decorated with quirky designs held in place with running stitch.
ANNE DELAUNEY

MATERIALS

Your own choice of fabrics, trimmings and embellishments is what makes a piece of appliqué work personal and unique. Select fabrics carefully and collect as many as possible to choose from. Look out for remnants at reduced prices and never throw left-over scraps of fabric away — you will find a use for them one day. Below are some other materials that may be useful for appliqué.

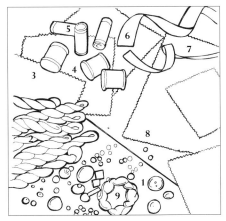

Beads and buttons These are both available in a wide range of colours, materials, sizes and shapes. Use buttons for decoration as well as fastenings, and to fasten quilts. Do not use buttons or beads on children's projects.

Binding tape This can be used for finishing edges.

Craft adhesive spray This is a spray-on glue that should be used sparingly and in a well-ventilated area. It is useful for fixing fabric on to card.

Double-sided adhesive tape This is used to stick fabric on to card or paper.

Embroidery threads These are available in many different thicknesses and textures. Stranded cotton threads can be separated; use two strands for fine work. Use embroidery threads to decorate or to secure fabrics.

Fabric glue This can be used instead of iron-on fusible bonding web to secure fabrics or trimmings together. It should be applied sparingly.

Fabrics Many kinds of fabric can be used in appliqué and you will often be able to use up remnants and other scraps. See the individual projects for advice on which fabrics are suitable for which technique or end use. Fabrics such as cotton can be dyed to obtain the desired colour for a particular design.

Felt Because this is a non-woven fabric, it is easy to cut and does not fray, making it very suitable for appliqué.

Iron-on fusible bonding web This is a very effective material for fixing two pieces of fabric together. It consists of a fine web of adhesive which is activated by the heat of an iron (see Basic Techniques). The result is washable and very durable.

Ribbons These are available in a wide variety of colours, materials, patterns and textures. Ribbons can be used functionally as drawstrings or as decoration.

Sewing threads These are used to machine-stitch fabrics together or to embellish designs.

Trimmings Many different kinds of trimmings are available, from simple braids to highly decorative pompoms and fringing.

Wool threads Tapestry wool thread is a strong matt embroidery thread which works very well on woollen fabrics; use a large-eyed tapestry needle. Knitting wool can also be used for embroidery or to make your own pompoms.

1 Beads and buttons
2 Embroidery threads
3 Fabrics
4 Sewing threads
5 Wool thread
6 Binding tape
7 Ribbon
8 Felt
9 Trimming

EQUIPMENT

V ERY LITTLE SPECIALIST EQUIPMENT IS NEEDED FOR APPLIQUÉ WORK. THE MOST IMPORTANT ITEM IS A SHARP PAIR OF SCISSORS. KEEP SCISSORS USED FOR CUTTING FABRICS AND THREADS SEPARATE FROM THOSE USED FOR PAPER AND CARD, OTHERWISE THEY WILL QUICKLY BECOME BLUNT.

Beading needle This needle is specially designed for stitching beads on to fabric. It is very fine and flexible, and particularly useful for tiny beads.

Dressmaker's pins These are used to pin fabrics together before tacking and stitching. Do not use blunt or rusty pins.

Dressmaker's scissors These should be used for cutting fabric only. Do not use them to cut paper or card, as this will blunt the edges.

Embroidery scissors These small scissors are very sharp, and are used to trim fabrics and cut threads. Do not use them to cut large areas of fabric.

Fading fabric marker This marker pen is very useful for drawing designs on to fabric. The marks will fade on contact with air or water (see Basic Techniques).

Iron Always check the temperature before ironing different fabrics. If possible, it is a good idea to use a separate iron for iron-on fusible bonding web.

Sewing machine A sewing machine with different stitch settings can be used for appliqué. Bobbins can be filled with a different coloured thread from the top thread to create decorative effects. Hand-sewing then can be used for decorative finishes.

Needle threader This is not essential, but does help when threading hand-sewing needles.

Pinking shears These specialist scissors have serrated blades, designed to cut fabrics so that the edges do not fray. They should not be used to cut paper.

Quilting pins These are longer than dressmaker's pins and can pin several layers of fabric and wadding together.

Pencil A pencil is useful for scaling up templates. To mark fabrics, use one of the materials listed here.

Ruler Use a metal ruler to draw straight lines on fabric. You may also need a ruler to enlarge the size of a template.

Safety pins These can be used to hold layers of fabric together. A safety pin is also needed to thread a drawstring through a fabric casing.

Tailor's chalk This is particularly useful to mark dark shades of fabric or those with uneven texture. It will rub off or disappear after washing.

Tape measure This is more flexible than a ruler and is also used to measure lengths of fabric.

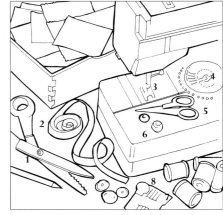

1 Pinking shears
2 Tape measure
3 Sewing machine
4 Quilting pins

5 Embroidery scissors
6 Bobbins
7 Needles
8 Needle threader

BASIC TECHNIQUES

THE BASIC IDEA BEHIND APPLIQUÉ IS A VERY SIMPLE ONE: SMALL PIECES OF FABRIC ARE APPLIED TO A BACKGROUND FABRIC TO CREATE DECORATIVE EFFECTS. HOWEVER, THE FOLLOWING TECHNIQUES WILL MAKE THE TASK EASIER AND WILL AID IN THE SUCCESS OF THE FINAL RESULT.

TRANSFERRING ORIGINAL DESIGNS

Tracing Templates

1 Place a piece of tracing paper over the shape. Draw round the shape, using a soft pencil.

2 Remove the tracing paper and turn it over. Scribble over the drawn lines as shown. Turn the tracing paper over again and place it on a piece of paper or thin card. Draw over the original drawing.

3 The shape should now be transferred to the paper or card. Go over it with a pencil if it is faint. Cut out the template.

Enlarging Templates

To enlarge a template, trace it on to graph paper following the above instructions. Decide the scale you want to enlarge it to then draw it again on a piece of larger-size graph paper. You can also enlarge templates on a photocopier.

Using a Fabric Marker

This is used to draw round a template to transfer the shape on to fabric. The marks made by a fading fabric marker gradually disappear on contact with air or water. You can also use a dressmaker's pencil.

Using Tailor's Chalk

This is useful for drawing designs on dark fabric or fabrics with an uneven texture. The chalk marks wash out or rub off.

IRON-ON FUSIBLE BONDING WEB

1 Set an iron to medium heat. Iron the bonding web on to the reverse side of the fabric.

2 Place the template on the backing paper of the bonding web. Draw round the shape, using a pencil, then cut out with a pair of scissors.

3 Remove the backing paper. Position the shape on the background fabric and iron it in place.

SATIN STITCH APPLIQUÉ

1 Draw the shape you wish to appliqué on a piece of fabric. Pin this on to the background fabric. Machine-stitch round the outline with straight stitch.

2 Using sharp scissors, trim the excess appliqué fabric, cutting close to the machine stitches.

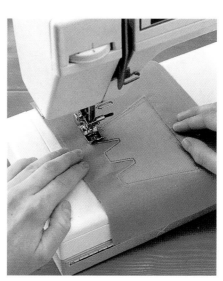

3 Machine-stitch over the first stitched outline and the edge of the shape, using satin stitch or an embroidery stitch.

TACKING OVER PAPER

1 Draw round the template on to a piece of fabric. Cut out, allowing an extra 5 mm (¼ in) seam allowance as shown.

2 Cut another paper template and place it on the back of the fabric shape. Tack the seam allowance over the edge of the paper, gently pulling the thread. Snip the fabric at points (for example, the inner point of a heart design) to help it fold over neatly.

3 Using a hot iron, iron over the back. Carefully remove the tacking stitches and the paper template.

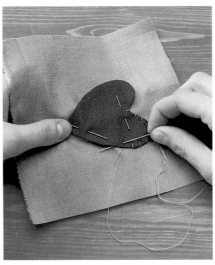

4 Pin the appliqué shape on to the background fabric. Hand- or machine-stitch round the edge.

REVERSE APPLIQUÉ

1 Draw round the template on to the main fabric. Draw another line approximately 5 mm (¼ in) inside the shape. Using sharp scissors, cut out the inner shape. Clip the 5 mm (¼ in) border at intervals then fold back to give a smooth outline. Press in place with a hot iron.

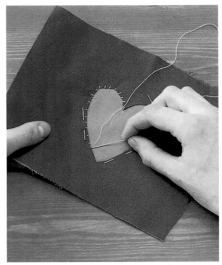

2 Place a contrasting fabric behind the outline shape and pin. Stitch round the edge of the shape.

CUTTING AND FOLDING EDGES

Curves

1 Using a sharp pair of scissors, snip into the dip in the curve up to the marked line. For the outside of the curve, cut out evenly spaced triangular notches of fabric.

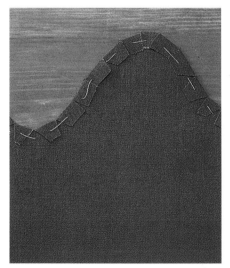

2 Fold over the edge along the marked line to the wrong side. Press with a hot iron then tack in place.

Points

1 To make a neat folded point, cut away the fabric around the point as shown.

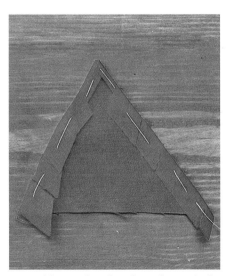

2 Fold over the edge along the marked line to the wrong side. Press with a hot iron then tack in place.

Inside Angles

1 At the inner point of the angle, snip the fabric up to the marked line.

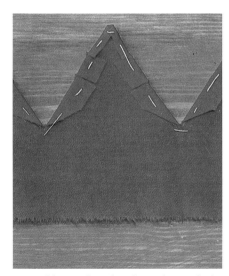

2 Fold over the edge along the marked line to the wrong side. Press with a hot iron then tack in place.

HAND STITCHES

Many different embroidery stitches can be used to attach and embellish appliqué shapes. These are some of the most commonly used hand stitches.

Stab Stitch

Bring the needle through the appliqué shape to the right side of the fabric. Start as close to or as far from the edge as you wish, depending on the size stitch required. Insert the needle into the background fabric to make a straight stitch.

French Knots

Bring the needle through the edge of the appliqué shape to the right side of the fabric. Holding the thread taut with your left hand, twist it several times around the needle. Still holding the thread taut, turn the needle and insert it back through the fabric at the same point. Pull gently on the needle to form a neat knot.

Feather Stitch

Starting at a point of the appliqué shape, bring the needle through the edge to the right side of the fabric. Make slanting stitches alternately to left and right, pulling the needle through the loop in the thread with each stitch. The stitches on the left will hold the shape in place.

Blanket Stitch

Work from left to right. Bring the needle through the appliqué shape to the right side of the fabric. Start as close to or as far from the edge as you wish, depending on whether you want a small or large stitch. Work a vertical stitch, catching thread under the tip of the needle as you draw it through the fabric. Space the stitches as evenly as possible.

Running Stitch

This is the simplest hand appliqué stitch. Bring the needle through the edge of the appliqué shape to the right side of the fabric. Insert the needle back in the fabric, leaving a gap approximately the same size as the stitch. The stitches can be any size. You can alternate the length of the stitches for decorative effect.

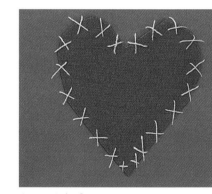

Cross Stitch

Bring the needle through the appliqué shape to the right side of the fabric. Start as close to or as far from the edge as you wish, depending on whether you want a small or large stitch. Insert the needle in the background fabric at an angle. Bring the needle out again on the appliqué shape immediately above this point. Make a stitch in the opposite direction to the first to form a cross.

HEART GIFT DECORATIONS

IT IS ALWAYS SUCH A TREAT TO RECEIVE A HANDMADE CARD AND MATCHING GIFT BOX. IT DOESN'T TAKE A HUGE AMOUNT OF TIME BUT THE RESULT IS SO SPECIAL. THE DESIGNS IN THIS PARTICULAR PROJECT ARE RICH AND SUMPTUOUS IN THEIR COLOURS AND FABRICS, WHICH MAKE THEM PERFECT FOR VALENTINE'S DAY BUT YOU COULD EASILY ADAPT THE IDEA TO SUIT OTHER SPECIAL OCCASIONS USING DIFFERENT COLOURS AND MOTIFS.

1 Cut out small hearts from scraps of organza, slightly smaller than the width of the organza ribbon. You will need approximately 20 hearts per metre (yard) length of ribbon.

2 Sew each heart on to the ribbon with running stitch and a contrasting thread that will show up against the fabric. Alternate the colours of the hearts along the length of the ribbon.

3 For the gift tag, cut a piece of coloured card to the size required and punch a hole at the top. ▶

MATERIALS AND EQUIPMENT YOU WILL NEED
DRESSMAKER'S SCISSORS • SCRAPS OF ORGANZA FABRICS • 1 CM (¾ IN) WIDE ORGANZA RIBBON • NEEDLE AND CONTRASTING
SEWING THREADS • PAPER SCISSORS • COLOURED CARD • HOLE PUNCH • EMBROIDERY THREADS • DOUBLE-SIDED TAPE • DECORATIVE CORD •
RULER • ASSORTED BEADS • SMALL GIFT BOX

4 Cut out a heart from organza and lay it on a square in a contrasting colour. Lay a third piece of organza over the top. Decorate with stitches using embroidery threads and tape to the tag.

6 For the greetings card, cut a piece of card 12 x 20 cm/4 x 5 in and fold in half. Use layers of organza to make up the main design, tacking the fabric together to hold in place.

7 Embellish the appliqué with decorative beads and stitches. Fix the appliqué design to the card with double-sided tape as before.

5 Cut a length of decorative cord and thread it through the punched hole. Tie the two ends in a knot.

8 For the gift box, assemble another appliqué design, using a combination of fabrics, and tacking them in place as before. Embellish with beads and decorative stitches and fix to the lid with tape.

KITCHEN COLLAGE

BLUE AND WHITE PLAIN AND PATTERNED FABRICS MAKE A VERY ATTRACTIVE FABRIC COLLAGE TO HANG ON THE WALL OF A KITCHEN OR BREAKFAST ROOM. DISPLAY THE PICTURE AS IT IS, AS A SMALL WALL HANGING, OR MOUNT IT IN A BOX FRAME SO THAT THE GLASS DOES NOT TOUCH THE APPLIQUÉ. THE COLLAGE WOULD ALSO WORK WELL IN SHADES OF ANOTHER COLOUR SUCH AS PINK OR GREEN, TO MATCH YOUR CHINA.

1 Cut two pieces of striped and plain fabric for the background to make an overall size of 34 x 42 cm (13½ x 16½ in). Machine-stitch together then cover the join with fabric tape. Fold under the edges by 1 cm (½ in) and press. Pin in place.

2 Iron fusible bonding web on to the reverse side of scraps of plain and patterned fabrics.

3 Trace the coffee pot and cup shapes from the back of the book and make templates (see Basic Techniques). Draw round the templates on to the bonding web and cut out.

MATERIALS AND EQUIPMENT YOU WILL NEED

DRESSMAKER'S SCISSORS • STRIPED AND PLAIN COTTON FABRICS • SEWING MACHINE AND MATCHING THREADS • FABRIC TAPE • IRON • DRESSMAKER'S PINS • IRON-ON FUSIBLE BONDING WEB • SCRAPS OF PLAIN AND PATTERNED FABRICS • TRACING PAPER • SOFT PENCIL • PAPER OR THIN CARD • PAPER SCISSORS • FADING FABRIC MARKER • EMBROIDERY SCISSORS • NEEDLE • EMBROIDERY THREADS • SMALL POMPOM (OPTIONAL) • BUTTONS • POMPOM TRIMMING • CRAFT KNIFE • MOUNT BOARD • DOUBLE-SIDED ADHESIVE TAPE

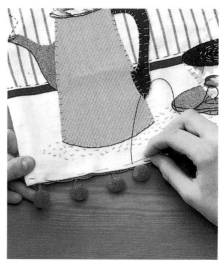

4 Peel off the backing paper from the coffee pot shapes and position on the fabric background. Iron in place. Repeat steps 1–4 for the coffee cup.

6 Work a swirl in running stitch on the top of the coffee cup to indicate steam. Stitch a wavy line of running stitches to indicate steam coming out of the spout of the coffee pot.

7 Stitch the pompom trimming along the bottom edge of the picture, as shown, so that the pompoms show on the right side. ▶

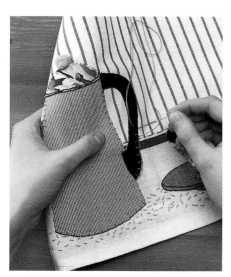

5 Decorate the appliqué with simple stitches. Outline some of the shapes with stab stitch or blanket stitch to accentuate them. Sew a small pompom or button on the lid of the coffee pot.

Simple decorative hand stitches complement the country-style design.

8 Hand-stitch neatly around the folded edges of the picture.

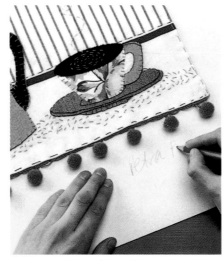

10 To frame the appliqué, cut a piece of mount board large enough to leave a wide border all around the picture. Attach the appliqué with a strip of double-sided tape along the top edge. Sign the picture in pencil.

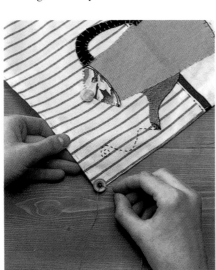

9 Sew a decorative button at each corner.

ALPHABET APRON

LARGE, BOLD SHAPES AND BRIGHT COLOURS ARE IDEAL FOR THIS CHILD'S APRON. THE COTTON FABRICS ARE STRONGLY STITCHED WITH DOUBLE SEAMS AND ZIGZAG STITCHING, SO THE APRON WILL STAND UP TO PLENTY OF WEAR AND FREQUENT WASHING.

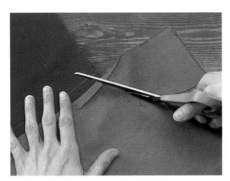

1 Fold the main fabrics in half width-ways. Wrong sides facing and matching centre points, pin together along one side. Machine-stitch, fold over the seam and stitch again. Mark curves at the top corners as shown and cut. Hem the edges.

3 Draw round the letters on to the backing of the fusible bonding web. Iron the bonding web on to the reverse of scraps of fabric, using different colours for adjacent letters, and cut out.

5 Using matching threads, zigzag-stitch round the edges of the letters.

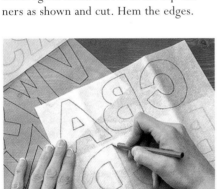

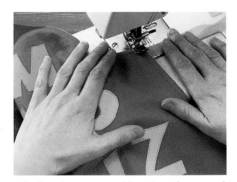

2 Enlarge the letters from the back of the book to approximately 7 cm (2¾ in) high (see Basic Techniques). Reverse and make templates.

4 Arrange the letters in five rows on the apron fabrics. Peel off the backing paper and iron in place.

6 Cut the tape or ribbon into four equal lengths. Machine-stitch to the top sides of the apron and either side of the neck edge. Knot the neck ties together and adjust to fit.

MATERIALS AND EQUIPMENT YOU WILL NEED
40 x 70 CM (16 x 28 IN) RED COTTON FABRIC • 30 x 40 CM (12 x 16 IN) BLUE COTTON FABRIC • DRESSMAKER'S PINS •
SEWING MACHINE AND MATCHING THREADS • TAILOR'S CHALK • DRESSMAKER'S SCISSORS • TRACING PAPER • SOFT PENCIL • GRAPH PAPER •
PAPER OR THIN CARD• PAPER SCISSORS • IRON-ON FUSIBLE BONDING WEB • IRON • SCRAPS OF COTTON FABRICS, IN BRIGHT COLOURS •
EMBROIDERY SCISSORS • 1.5 M (60 IN) OF 2 CM (¾ IN) WIDE YELLOW FABRIC TAPE OR RIBBON

HANDS AND HEARTS THROW

USE YOUR OWN HAND AS THE TEMPLATE FOR THIS TRADITIONAL QUILTED THROW. THE SYMBOLIC MOTIFS AND CHECK COTTON FABRICS ARE BORROWED FROM AMERICAN FOLK DESIGNS, GENERATING A FEELING OF WARMTH AND HOSPITALITY. IN THIS PROJECT, THE BUTTONS ARE NOT SIMPLY FOR DECORATION; THEY SERVE TO QUILT THE LAYERS OF FABRIC TOGETHER. LAY THE THROW OUT FLAT FOR QUILTING AND WORK FROM THE CENTRE OUTWARDS.

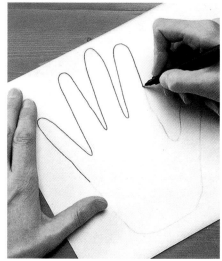

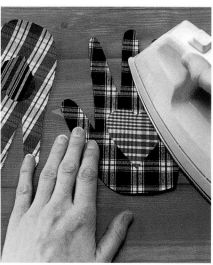

1 Draw round your hand in pencil. Draw round the outline again in felt pen, simplifying the shape.

2 Trace the hand shape and transfer it on to the paper side of the fusible bonding web (see Basic Techniques). Iron the bonding web on to the reverse of a piece of check fabric and cut out.

3 Draw a heart shape on to bonding web. Iron the bonding web on to the reverse of a piece of contrasting fabric and cut out. Iron the heart on to the hand as shown. ▶

MATERIALS AND EQUIPMENT YOU WILL NEED

SOFT PENCIL • PAPER • FELT-TIP PEN • TRACING PAPER • IRON-ON FUSIBLE BONDING WEB • DRESSMAKER'S SCISSORS • IRON • SCRAPS OF CHECK COTTON FABRICS, IN DIFFERENT COLOURS • 1.5 M (60 IN) SQUARE OF HEAVY CREAM COTTON FABRIC • DRESSMAKER'S PINS • SEWING MACHINE AND MATCHING THREADS • 1.6 M (64 IN) SQUARE OF CHECK COTTON FABRIC, FOR THE BACKING • 1.5 M (60 IN) SQUARE OF POLYESTER WADDING • SAFETY PINS • STRANDED COTTON EMBROIDERY THREADS • NEEDLE • ASSORTED BUTTONS

4 Make 11 more hand shapes, varying the fabrics. Iron a heart shape on to each hand, as in step 3. Peel off the backing paper.

6 Using matching threads, machine-stitch around both the hand and the heart shapes in a close zigzag stitch.

8 Press under 1 cm (½ in) of the backing fabric all round. Fold over to the right side of the throw and press under 5 cm (2 in) to make a border. Pin, then machine-stitch, mitring the corners. Using six strands of embroidery thread, sew buttons between the hand shapes.

5 Position the hands on the cream fabric, leaving a border of approximately 25 cm (10 in) all round. Pin in place then iron.

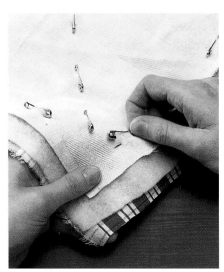

7 Lay the backing fabric out flat, with the wrong side facing upwards. Centre the wadding on top. Lay the appliqué right side up on top. Trim the wadding so that the backing fabric is 6 cm (2½ in) larger all round. Secure the three layers together with safety pins.

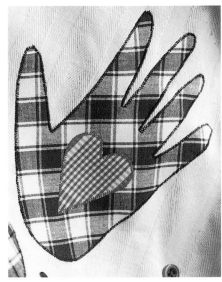

The secret to working with different patterns is to choose a limited range of colours.

ANGEL STOCKING

DIFFERENT SHADES OF DARK BLUE AND FADED DENIM WORK VERY WELL TOGETHER, SHOWING THAT YOU DO NOT ALWAYS NEED TO USE BRIGHT OR CONTRASTING COLOURS IN APPLIQUÉ. THIS IS A GOOD WAY TO RECYCLE OLD JEANS AND DENIM SHIRTS. MAKE THE CHRISTMAS STOCKING AS LARGE OR AS SMALL AS YOU WISH — THE DENIM FABRIC IS CERTAINLY STRONG ENOUGH TO CARRY THE WEIGHT OF PLENTY OF PRESENTS!

1 Trace the angel shapes at the back of the book and make templates (see Basic Techniques). Iron fusible bonding web on to the back of scraps of denim. Draw round the templates on to the bonding web and cut out.

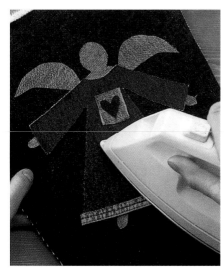

2 Draw a large stocking shape on a piece of paper and cut out to make a template. Draw round the template on to two pieces of denim and cut out. Remove the backing paper from the bonding web. Position the appliqué shapes on the right side of one stocking piece and iron it in place.

3 Decorate the angel with different embroidery stitches, as shown. Stitch the features on the face and the hair.

4 Sew buttons around the angel and scattered over the rest of the stocking. ▶

MATERIALS AND EQUIPMENT YOU WILL NEED

TRACING PAPER • SOFT PENCIL • PAPER OR THIN CARD • PAPER SCISSORS • IRON • IRON-ON FUSIBLE BONDING WEB • SCRAPS OF DENIM, IN DIFFERENT SHADES • DRESSMAKER'S PENCIL OR FADING FABRIC MARKER • DRESSMAKER'S SCISSORS • NEEDLE • EMBROIDERY THREADS • BUTTONS • DRESSMAKER'S PINS • RIBBON • SEWING MACHINE AND MATCHING THREADS • PINKING SHEARS • GINGHAM FABRIC

5 Right sides facing, pin the two stocking pieces together, leaving the top edge open. Cut a 12 cm (4¾ in) length of ribbon, fold in half and trap between the two stocking pieces on one side, approximately 6 cm (2½ in) below the top. Machine-stitch the pieces, leaving a 1 cm (½ in) seam. Neaten the raw edges with pinking shears.

7 Place the denim stocking inside the lining stocking, matching the top raw edges. Pin the denim and lining together around the top opening. Machine-stitch, leaving a 1 cm (½ in) seam.

6 For the lining, use pinking shears to cut two stocking shapes from gingham fabric. Right sides facing, pin together, leaving the top edge open. Machine-stitch, leaving a 1 cm (½ in) seam and a 15 cm (6 in) gap along one side.

8 Push the denim stocking through the gap in the lining then push the lining inside the denim stocking. Slip-stitch the gap. Stitch a line of running stitch around the top edge of the stocking. Make up additional stockings in the same way, varying the designs.

TOY BAG

TIDY AWAY TOYS OR LAUNDRY IN THIS STRONG COTTON DRILL BAG. THE APPLIQUÉ DOG MOTIF IS MADE OF DIFFERENT SCRAPS OF LEFT-OVER FABRICS, IRONED IN PLACE WITH FUSIBLE BONDING WEB. FOR WET WASHING OR SPORTS CLOTHES, YOU CAN MAKE A PLASTIC LINING TO GO INSIDE THE BAG.

1 Right sides facing, fold the cotton drill fabric in half widthways. Machine-stitch the side seams, stopping 25 cm (10 in) from the top. Reverse-stitch to reinforce the stitching. Fold back the top edges by 10 cm (4 in) so that the right sides are facing. Stitch, leaving a 1 cm (½ in) seam allowance, and fold right side out. Turn the bag right side out.

2 To make the casings for the ribbon ties, cut two strips of contrasting fabric. Fold in half lengthways and press. Open out then fold the sides into the centre. Fold over each end. Position one on each side of the bag and stitch in place leaving open at one end. Cut a second piece of contrasting fabric 23 x 21 cm (9 x 8¼ in). Fold under 6 mm (¼ in) on each side and press.

3 Trace the dog shapes from the back of the book and make templates (see Basic Techniques). Iron the fusible bonding web on to the reverse side of scraps of different fabrics. Draw round the templates on to the bonding web and cut out. Position the dog shapes on the fabric panel and iron in place.

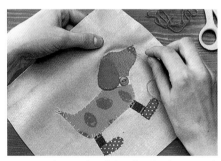

4 Stitch on a bead for the dog's eye and embroider French knots for the nose. Stitch a button on the collar.

5 Position the panel on one side of the bag and pin in place. Machine-stitch. Stitch a button to each corner by hand.

6 Cut the ribbon in half. Fasten a safety pin to one end of one ribbon then thread it through the casing. Secure at either end with pins. Thread the second ribbon through the other casing and pin the ends. Cut each felt square into two triangles. Trap each pair of ribbon ends between two triangles then stitch all around the edge in running stitch.

MATERIALS AND EQUIPMENT YOU WILL NEED

DRESSMAKER'S SCISSORS • 50 x 150 CM (20 x 60 IN) COTTON DRILL FABRIC, FOR THE BAG • SEWING MACHINE AND MATCHING THREADS • TWO PLAIN, CONTRASTING FABRICS • IRON • TRACING PAPER • SOFT PENCIL • PAPER OR THIN CARD • PAPER SCISSORS • IRON-ON FUSIBLE BONDING WEB • SCRAPS OF DIFFERENT FABRICS • NEEDLE AND EMBROIDERY THREADS • EMBROIDERY SCISSORS • BEAD • BUTTONS • DRESSMAKER'S PINS • 3 M (3 YD) NARROW RIBBON • SAFETY PINS • TWO 10 CM (4 IN) SQUARES OF FELT, IN DIFFERENT COLOURS

HEARTS AND STARS BLANKET

THIS BRIGHTLY DECORATED BLANKET IS CERTAIN TO CHEER YOU UP AS WELL AS KEEPING YOU WARM. ITS APPEAL LIES IN THE TONING ICE-CREAM COLOURS AND TEXTURED FABRIC. THE APPLIQUÉ MOTIFS ARE ALL MADE OF BLANKET FABRIC, STITCHED BY HAND WITH WOOL THREADS WHICH GIVE A BOLD, CHUNKY FEEL TO THE DESIGN. IF YOU ARE MAKING THE BLANKET FOR A CHILD, LEAVE OUT THE BEADS AND BUTTONS AND USE EXTRA EMBROIDERY STITCHES AS EMBELLISHMENT INSTEAD.

1 Trace the heart and star templates from the back of the book and make templates (see Basic Techniques). Draw round the templates on to the coloured blanket fabrics, using a fading fabric marker and cut out.

2 Embroider some of the hearts and stars with French knots, using wool in contrasting colours (see Basic Techniques).

3 Embroider the remaining hearts and stars with decorative cross stitches in contrasting colours.

MATERIALS AND EQUIPMENT YOU WILL NEED

TRACING PAPER • SOFT PENCIL • PAPER OR THIN CARD • PAPER SCISSORS • SCRAPS OF COLOURED BLANKET FABRIC • FADING FABRIC MARKER •
DRESSMAKER'S SCISSORS • TAPESTRY NEEDLE • TAPESTRY WOOL OR KNITTING WOOL, IN DIFFERENT COLOURS • ASSORTED BEADS •
SMALL COLOURED BUTTONS • BLANKET • DRESSMAKER'S PINS

4 Stitch assorted beads on to some of the appliqué shapes. Be careful to attach them securely.

6 Work a line of decorative running stitch along each end of the blanket in contrasting wool.

7 Lay the blanket out flat and position the heart and star shapes in a pleasing arrangement. Pin them in place. ▶

5 Stitch buttons to the other shapes and embroider with more decorative stitches, using wool threads.

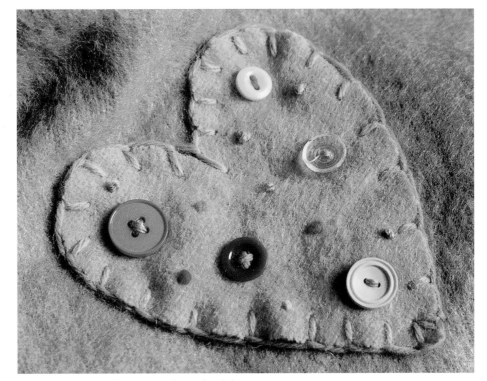

Buttons and beads add interest to the appliqué shape.

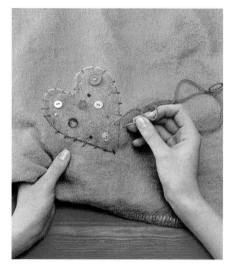

8 Stitch some of the shapes on to the blanket, using stab stitch (see Basic Techniques) and a contrasting wool.

10 Fill in the background with individual large cross stitches.

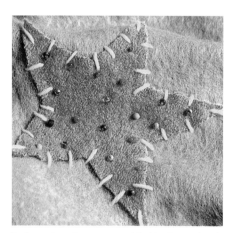

Stab stitch is decorative and holds the appliqué shape in place.

9 Stitch the remaining shapes on to the blanket, using blanket stitch.

MOSAIC VELVET CUSHION

THIS RICH VELVET CUSHION COVER IS A CLEVER WAY TO USE SCRAPS OF FABRIC. THE TRIANGULAR SHAPES AND DECORATIVE EMBROIDERY ARE REMINISCENT OF CRAZY PATCHWORK, WHICH WAS VERY POPULAR IN THE VICTORIAN ERA. THE AIM AT THE TIME WAS TO CREATE A RANDOM DESIGN, HENCE THE NAME. TO CREATE A MOSAIC EFFECT, THE PIECES MAY BE ARRANGED MORE REGULARLY. TO MAKE UP THE CUSHION, SEE THE INLAID BOAT CUSHION PROJECT.

1 Measure the cushion pad. For the cushion front, cut a piece of velvet to this size plus 2 cm (¾ in) all round. Cut triangles in different sizes from scraps of contrasting velvet. Press under the edges of the triangles by 7 mm (⅜ in), ensuring that the edges are straight.

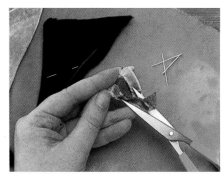

2 Trim the excess fabric at the corners. Tack around the edge of each triangle. Arrange the triangles on the background velvet and pin in place.

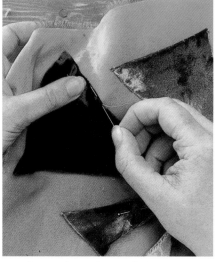

3 Slip-stitch neatly round the edge of each triangle. Remove tacking.

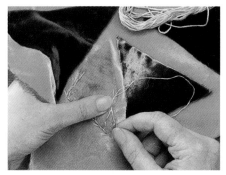

4 Outline some of the triangles with feather stitch, using contrasting embroidery threads.

5 Stitch round the edge of other triangles with blanket stitch and other decorative embroidery stitches. Make up the cushion and insert the pad.

MATERIALS AND EQUIPMENT YOU WILL NEED

TAPE MEASURE • CUSHION PAD • DRESSMAKER'S SCISSORS • VELVET • SCRAPS OF CONTRASTING VELVET • IRON • EMBROIDERY SCISSORS • NEEDLE • TACKING THREAD • DRESSMAKER'S PINS • MATCHING SEWING THREADS • EMBROIDERY THREADS

COUNTRY CANDLESHADES

NATURAL-COLOURED LINEN AND TEXTURED APPLIQUÉ FABRICS COMPLEMENT ONE ANOTHER TO CREATE THESE CHARMING CANDLESHADES. FRAY THE EDGES OF THE FABRICS AND DECORATE THE DESIGN WITH PEARL BUTTONS AND EMBROIDERY STITCHES TO COMPLETE THE EFFECT. IN THIS PROJECT, THE CARD TEMPLATE IS USED IN THE FINISHED CANDLESHADE TO BACK THE APPLIQUÉ. DO NOT LEAVE THE CANDLESHADES UNATTENDED AT ANY TIME WHEN IN USE.

1 Enlarge the candleshade shape from the back of the book so that it measures 10 cm (4 in) high (see Basic Techniques). Transfer on to thin card and cut out to make a template.

3 Draw small heart shapes on scraps of fabric and cut out. Cut small squares of fabric and fray the edges slightly. Appliqué some of the heart shapes through the squares on to the candleshade fabric, using stab stitch and two strands of embroidery thread.

5 Place the appliquéd shade face down on a protected surface and spray lightly with adhesive. Place the card template on top. Fold the edges of the linen to the inside, smoothing the fabric as you go.

2 Using a fabric marker, draw round the template on to the linen fabric. Cut out the fabric, adding an extra 1.5 cm (⅝ in) for turnings.

4 Add the single heart shapes. Sew pearl buttons in the middle of some of the appliqué hearts and scattered over the background. Vary the stitches used.

6 Fold in the raw edge and glue lightly. Bend the candleshade into shape and hold together with paperclips until the glue is dry. Slip-stitch the joined edge if necessary, stitching through the card.

MATERIALS AND EQUIPMENT YOU WILL NEED

TRACING PAPER • SOFT PENCIL • GRAPH PAPER • THIN CARD • PAPER SCISSORS • FADING FABRIC MARKER •
25 x 35 CM (10 x 14 IN) NATURAL-COLOURED LINEN • DRESSMAKER'S SCISSORS • SCRAPS OF NATURAL-COLOURED AND TEXTURED FABRICS •
EMBROIDERY SCISSORS • NEEDLE • STRANDED COTTON EMBROIDERY THREADS • SMALL PEARL BUTTONS • CRAFT ADHESIVE SPRAY •
FABRIC GLUE • PAPERCLIPS

CHRISTMAS TREE STARS

RED AND GREEN, THE TRADITIONAL FESTIVE COLOURS, ARE MIXED AND MATCHED IN THESE TWO COMPLEMENTARY DESIGNS. BOTH ARE SIMPLE AND QUICK TO MAKE BY HAND, USING SMALL, NEAT RUNNING STITCHES. AS AN ALTERNATIVE TO THIS BOLD, COORDINATED EFFECT, YOU CAN EXPERIMENT WITH A VARIETY OF DIFFERENT COLOURS OR EMBELLISH THE CHRISTMAS DECORATIONS WITH BEADS, SEQUINS AND SHINY EMBROIDERY THREADS.

1 Draw a star shape on to paper or thin card and make a template. Using tailor's chalk, draw round the template on to felt.

2 Cut equal numbers of red and green stars from the felt.

3 Using the point of the scissors, pierce one of the red stars 5 mm (⅕ in) from the edge. Cut out a smaller star, leaving a 5 mm (⅕ in) border all round. ▶

MATERIALS AND EQUIPMENT YOU WILL NEED

SOFT PENCIL • PAPER OR THIN CARD • PAPER SCISSORS • TAILOR'S CHALK • RED AND GREEN FELT • EMBROIDERY SCISSORS •
NEEDLE AND MATCHING THREADS • SCRAPS OF PATTERNED FABRIC • RIBBON

4 Stitch the red border to one of the green stars with small, even running stitches and matching thread.

5 Centre a small red star cut out in step 3 on a green star. Stitch in place.

6 Place the stars from steps 4 and 5 together, sandwiching a plain red star in the middle. Stitch the three stars together at the inner points, as shown.

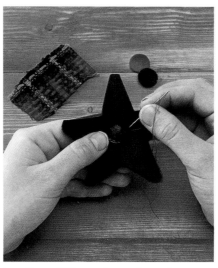

7 For a different decoration, take a green felt star and cut a small circle from the centre. Place on top of a red star, with a small piece of patterned fabric showing through the hole. Stitch neatly round the hole in running stitch.

8 Stitch the two stars together around the edges with stab stitch.

9 Use a loop of ribbon for hanging. Alternatively, wrap sewing thread around all four fingers. Stitch a loop on to a point of each star with small stitches.

INLAID BOAT CUSHION

INLAID APPLIQUÉ IS A VARIATION ON THE BASIC TECHNIQUE IN WHICH THE DESIGN IS DRAWN ON THE BACKGROUND FABRIC AND CUT OUT, LEAVING OPEN SPACES. THE CUT-OUT SHAPES ARE THEN PLACED ON FABRICS IN CONTRASTING COLOURS, CUT OUT AGAIN AND THE CONTRASTING COLOURS ARE USED TO FILL THE SPACES. THIS TECHNIQUE IS BEST SUITED TO FABRICS OF THE SAME THICKNESS WHICH DO NOT FRAY, SUCH AS BLANKET AND HEAVY WOOLLEN FABRICS.

1 Trace the templates from the back of the book and enlarge to the size required (see Basic Techniques). Measure the cushion pad and cut out a piece of blanket fabric to this size plus 2 cm (¾ in) all round. Position the templates on the main fabric. Using a fabric marker, draw round the templates on the reverse of the fabric.

2 Using a sharp pair of scissors, cut out the shapes from the main fabric.

3 Place each cut-out shape on a piece of different-coloured blanket fabric, pin and cut out. ▶

MATERIALS AND EQUIPMENT YOU WILL NEED

TRACING PAPER • SOFT PENCIL • PAPER OR THIN CARD • PAPER SCISSORS • TAPE MEASURE • SQUARE CUSHION PAD • DRESSMAKER'S SCISSORS •
BLANKET FABRICS IN DIFFERENT COLOURS • FADING FABRIC MARKER • DRESSMAKER'S PINS • EMBROIDERY SCISSORS •
CONTRASTING COTTON FABRICS FOR THE BACK • FABRIC GLUE AND BRUSH • TAPESTRY NEEDLE • WOOL THREADS • NEEDLE AND SEWING THREAD •
SCRAP OF FELT • CORD • LARGE BUTTON • BEADS • NARROW RIBBON • IRON • SEWING MACHINE • FOUR POMPOMS

4 Cut a piece of cotton fabric larger than the boat design. Glue on to the back of the piece in step 1, behind the cut-out areas.

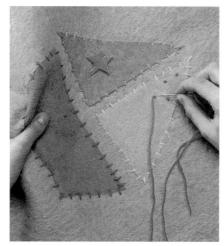

6 Use coloured wool threads to decorate the sails with French knots (see Basic Techniques) and an appliqué star cut from a scrap of felt.

8 To line the design, cut a piece of cotton fabric the same size as the cushion front and place it on the reverse of the appliqué. For the cushion back, cut two pieces of fabric in different colours, to the width of the front but two-thirds of the length. Fold under and press a 1 cm (½ in) double hem on both opening edges; machine-stitch. Right sides facing, place the cushion front on the two overlapping back pieces and machine-stitch all round. Turn the cushion cover right side out. Hand-stitch a pompom to each corner.

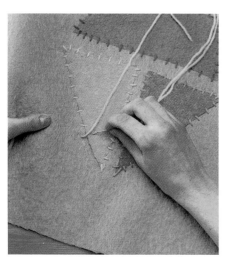

5 Place the coloured cut-out shapes in the openings and pin in place. Using coloured wool threads, hand-stitch the shapes to the surrounding blanket with large stab stitches.

7 Cut a small fabric rectangle for the cabin and appliqué in place as shown. Using sewing thread, stitch on a piece of cord for the mast, add a large button at the top, then sew a bead to the bottom corner of each sail. Stitch ribbon across the boat's hull, using cross stitch.

SHADOW-APPLIQUÉ SCARF

THIS DELICATE, FLOATY SCARF IS MADE OF LAYERS OF CHIFFON, WITH SQUARES OF FABRIC APPLIQUÉD AT RANDOM WITH A LEAF-LIKE MOTIF. CHIFFON IS RATHER A SLIPPERY FABRIC SO IT PAYS TO TACK THE LAYERS SECURELY TOGETHER BEFORE MACHINE STITCHING. THE RAW EDGES OF THE APPLIQUÉ ARE FINISHED WITH DECORATIVE EMBROIDERY STITCHES, AND THE EDGES OF THE SCARF ARE ROLLED AND STITCHED BY HAND.

1 Cut a piece of chiffon 30 x 105 cm (12 x 41½ in). Press in half lengthways, open out then press folds 15 cm (6 in) along length. Cut 17 cm (6¾ in) squares of chiffon. Tack one square to the reverse of the main piece, using fold lines as a guide.

3 Make a leaf and circle template. Using a fabric marker, draw round the templates several times on to different squares of chiffon.

5 Using doubled sewing thread, stitch along all the machine-stitched lines in feather stitch to cover the raw edges.

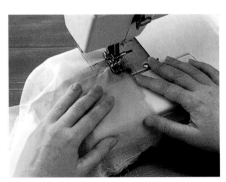

2 Following the fold lines, machine-stitch the square in place. Trim the excess fabric 3 mm (⅛ in) outside the stitch line. Repeat along the scarf.

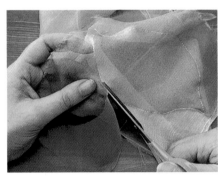

4 Pin each appliqué square on to a contrasting square on the scarf, choosing squares at random. Tack, then machine-stitch around the shape. Trim the excess fabric 3 mm (⅛ in) outside the stitch line.

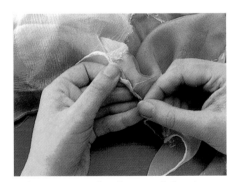

6 Using your forefinger and thumb, carefully roll each edge of the scarf until the raw edges are concealed. Stitch in place with slip stitch.

MATERIALS AND EQUIPMENT YOU WILL NEED

DRESSMAKER'S SCISSORS • CHIFFON, IN THREE DIFFERENT COLOURS • IRON • DRESSMAKER'S PINS • NEEDLE • TACKING THREAD • SEWING MACHINE AND MATCHING THREADS • SOFT PENCIL • PAPER OR THIN CARD • PAPER SCISSORS • FADING FABRIC MARKER • EMBROIDERY SCISSORS

HEART-WARMING HATS

Brighten up a cold winter's day with these cheerful appliqué hearts and flowers, stitched on to two ready-made woollen hats and a scarf. Decorate the simple shapes with beads, buttons and embroidery threads, using oddments from your needlework box. Use a cool iron for woollen fabrics and take care not to stretch or distort them when you stitch on the appliqué shapes.

1 For the button heart hat, draw a large heart shape on paper or card and cut out to make a template. Draw round the template on to a piece of fusible bonding web. Iron on to a piece of felt and cut out.

2 Position the heart on the front of the hat. Iron in place, using a cool iron.

3 Using embroidery thread in a contrasting colour, stitch around the edge of the heart in stab stitch.

4 Decorate the heart with buttons in different sizes and colours.

MATERIALS AND EQUIPMENT YOU WILL NEED

Pencil • Paper or thin card • Paper scissors • Iron-on fusible bonding web • Embroidery scissors • Iron • Scraps of felt • Woollen hats • Needle • Embroidery threads • Various buttons, in different sizes and colours • Fading fabric marker • Woollen scarf • Beading needle • Small glass beads • Knitting wool • String

5 For the flowery scarf, draw two flower shapes on to paper or thin card and cut out. Using a fabric marker, draw round both templates on to scraps of felt.

7 Thread a beading needle and knot the end of the thread. Thread on a few beads and stitch down in the centre of a flower. Decorate all the flowers in the same way.

9 For the heart hat with pompom, draw two heart shapes on to paper or card, one smaller than the other. Cut out to make templates. Iron fusible bonding web on to scraps of felt. Draw round the templates several times on to the bonding web and cut out. Place the larger heart shapes round the edge of the hat and iron in place, then place smaller hearts on top and iron in place.

6 Position the flowers at either end of the scarf. Using embroidery threads, attach with a few stitches in the centre of each flower.

8 Stitch short lengths of embroidery thread in the spaces between the flowers, using a single running stitch. Tie the ends in a double knot then trim.

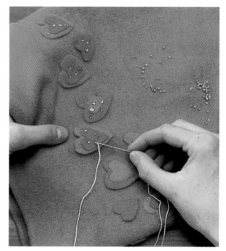

10 Decorate the hearts with stitches and beads, using embroidery threads in contrasting colours. ▶

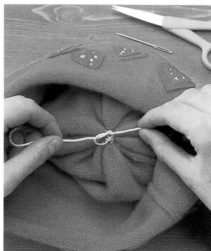

11 To make the pompom, cut two 12 cm (4¾ in) diameter circles in card. Cut out a 4 cm (1½ in) diameter circle from the centre of each. Place the two together and wrap knitting wool around them and through the hole until the central hole is filled. Insert the blades of a sharp pair of scissors between the two pieces of card and cut the wool. Pass a piece of string between the two pieces of card and knot. Remove the card circles.

12 Fluff up the pompom to make a ball and trim. Stitch to the top of the hat.

A heart embellished with buttons makes a contemporary decoration.

SPOTTED CUSHION

THE DIFFERENT TEXTURES OF TOWELLING, VELVET AND WOOL COME TOGETHER IN THIS VERY ORIGINAL APPLIQUÉ CUSHION. THE CIRCLES ARE CUT OUT AND THEN FILLED IN WITH DIFFERENT FABRICS FROM BEHIND, USING THE REVERSE APPLIQUÉ TECHNIQUE (SEE BASIC TECHNIQUES). THE STITCHING IN THIS PROJECT IS DONE BY MACHINE, EXCEPT FOR THE POMPOM EDGING. IF YOU CANNOT FIND A TRIMMING IN A SUITABLE COLOUR, TRY DYEING ONE WITH FABRIC DYE.

1 Measure the cushion pad and cut a piece of woollen fabric to this size plus 2 cm (¾ in) all round. Using tailor's chalk, draw round a circular object on to six squares of the same fabric, as shown.

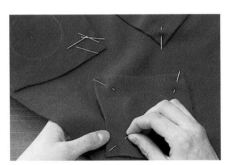

2 Position the squares on the large piece of woollen fabric, not too close to the edge. Pin in place.

3 Machine-stitch round each circle in a straight stitch. Remove the pins.

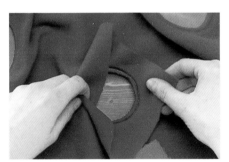

4 Using sharp scissors, cut through both layers of fabric inside each circle close to the stitching. Push the rest of the fabric square through the hole and press in place. Cut out squares of velvet and towelling in different colours, larger than the holes. Pin a fabric square behind each hole then machine-stitch round the edge of the circle.

5 To make the cushion back, cut two pieces of fabric in different colours, to the width of the front and two-thirds of the length. Use pinking shears if desired. Fold under and press a 1 cm (½ in) double hem on both opening edges. Machine-stitch. Right sides facing, place the cushion front on the two overlapping back pieces and stitch all round.

6 Turn the cushion cover right side out. Hand-stitch the pompom trimming round the edge. Insert the cushion pad.

MATERIALS AND EQUIPMENT YOU WILL NEED

TAPE MEASURE • CUSHION PAD • DRESSMAKER'S SCISSORS • WOOLLEN FABRIC • TAILOR'S CHALK • CIRCULAR TEMPLATE • DRESSMAKER'S PINS • SEWING MACHINE AND MATCHING THREADS • EMBROIDERY SCISSORS • IRON • SCRAPS OF VELVET AND TOWELLING, IN DIFFERENT COLOURS • TWO FABRICS IN DIFFERENT COLOURS, FOR THE BACK • PINKING SHEARS (OPTIONAL) • POMPOM TRIMMING • NEEDLE AND MATCHING THREAD

GARDENER'S APRON

MODERN TECHNOLOGY AND TRADITIONAL CRAFT MEET IN THIS STRIKING DESIGN, WHICH MAKES USE OF A HEAT-TRANSFER MACHINE AT A PHOTOCOPYING SHOP. YOU CAN USE OTHER IMAGES IN MAGAZINES OR PHOTOGRAPHS TO CREATE YOUR OWN PERSONALIZED APRON, PERHAPS FOR A COOK OR ARTIST. YOU CAN USE IMAGE-TRANSFER GEL INSTEAD OF THE HEAT-TRANSFER MACHINE IN STEP 2. ALLOW THE PRINTS TO COOL AND DRY BEFORE FOLDING OR MOVING THEM.

1 Cut a selection of flower images out of magazines and photographs. Glue them lightly on to the A4 paper.

3 Using a cool iron, iron fusible bonding web on to the reverse of the flower print fabric.

4 Cut out the flower shapes and arrange on the apron. Peel off the backing paper and iron in place, using a cool iron and a piece of cotton fabric.

2 Take the cotton fabric to a photocopying shop with a heat-transfer machine. Transfer the images to the fabric. Leave to cool.

5 Stitch around the outline of each flower, using stab stitch and matching sewing threads.

MATERIALS AND EQUIPMENT YOU WILL NEED

PAPER SCISSORS • FLOWER IMAGES FROM MAGAZINES OR PHOTOGRAPHS • PAPER GLUE • SHEET OF A4 PAPER • WHITE COTTON FABRIC • IRON •
IRON-ON FUSIBLE BONDING WEB • EMBROIDERY SCISSORS • APRON • NEEDLE • MATCHING SEWING THREADS

FELT CURTAIN

THIS BOLD ABSTRACT DESIGN CAN BRIGHTEN A WINDOW OR BE USED TO DISGUISE AN UNTIDY CORNER. MACHINE-STITCHED STRIPES ARE OVERLAID WITH COLOURFUL CIRCLES, ATTACHED WITH LARGE HAND STITCHES. THE FELT FABRICS WILL NOT FRAY SO THERE IS NO NEED TO WORRY ABOUT FINISHING THE EDGES OF ANY OF THE SHAPES. MAKE THE CURTAIN TO FIT THE AREA DESIRED; A LARGER VERSION WOULD MAKE A GOOD ROOM DIVIDER.

1 Measure the blue felt and cut to the size of curtain required. Cut the cream felt into strips 4 cm (1½ in) wide then pin on to the blue felt 4 cm (1½ in) apart. Using blue thread, machine-stitch down each side.

2 To make hanging loops, cut a piece of blue felt 12 cm (4¾ in) wide and the width of the curtain. Using tailor's chalk, mark every 4 cm (1½ in). Cut down each marked line to the last then cut out every alternate bar. Leaving a 4 cm (1½ in)

3 Pin the hanging loops to the top of the curtain at the back then stitch. ▶

MATERIALS AND EQUIPMENT YOU WILL NEED
TAPE MEASURE • BLUE FELT • DRESSMAKER'S SCISSORS • METAL RULER • CREAM FELT • DRESSMAKER'S PINS •
SEWING MACHINE AND MATCHING THREADS • TAILOR'S CHALK • EMBROIDERY SCISSORS • SCRAPS OF COLOURED FELT •
CUTTING COMPASS AND MAT (OPTIONAL) • NEEDLE • EMBROIDERY THREADS

4 Cut out circles of coloured felt, using a cutting compass and mat or scissors. Cut out a hole in each circle and swap the colours.

6 Pin the circles on to the right side of the curtain. Hand-stitch in place, using contrasting threads and large, simple stitches.

8 For the border, cut three lengths of blue felt 4 cm (1½ in) wide; two lengths for the sides and one for the bottom of the curtain. Pin and machine-stitch in place.

5 Using contrasting threads and large, simple stitches, stitch the contrasting centres into the circles.

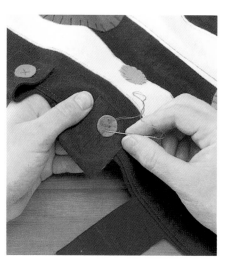

7 Fold the hanging loops over to the front of the curtain. Stitch in place with small felt circles, using a single large cross stitch.

BRODERIE PERSE TABLECLOTH

THE IDEA OF CUTTING MOTIFS OUT OF PRINTED FABRICS AND APPLIQUÉING THEM ON TO PLAIN FABRIC CAN BE SEEN IN EARLY QUILTS. IMPORTED CHINTZ FABRICS FROM THE FAR EAST WERE TOO HIGHLY PRIZED TO BE THROWN AWAY AFTER USE, SO THE BEST PORTIONS WERE SAVED AND RECYCLED IN THIS WAY. FOR THE APPLIQUÉ MOTIFS, CHOOSE FABRICS WHICH DO NOT FRAY OR PAINT THE EDGES WITH ANTI-FRAYING SOLUTION, AVAILABLE FROM SPECIALIST CRAFT SHOPS.

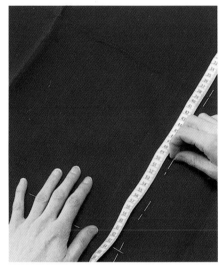 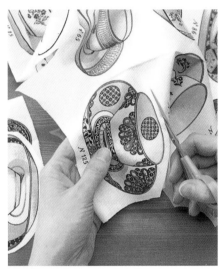 

1 Fold the tablecloth into quarters and mark 25 cm (10 in) from the centre on each crease with a pin. Unfold the tablecloth. Using a tape measure and the pins as a guide, pin a 50 cm (20 in) square in the centre.

2 Use a pair of embroidery scissors to cut motifs from the printed fabric. The motifs can be cut out fairly roughly at this stage.

3 Iron fusible bonding web on to the reverse of the motifs. Cut them out carefully, as close to the outlines as possible. If necessary, treat the edges with anti-fraying solution. ▶

MATERIALS AND EQUIPMENT YOU WILL NEED

PLAIN TABLECLOTH • TAPE MEASURE • DRESSMAKER'S PINS • EMBROIDERY SCISSORS • PRINTED FABRIC, WITH SUITABLE MOTIFS • IRON •
IRON-ON FUSIBLE BONDING WEB • ANTI-FRAYING SOLUTION (OPTIONAL) • CARD • SEWING MACHINE AND MATCHING SEWING THREADS • NAPKINS

4 Arrange some of the motifs along the inside edge of the marked square.

6 Using matching threads, machine-stitch around the edge of each motif with a close zigzag stitch.

5 Arrange the rest of the motifs within the marked square, in a more random pattern. Slip a piece of card under the tablecloth to protect your work surface. Peel off the backing paper and iron the motifs in place.

7 To make matching napkins, appliqué single motifs to the corners, using fusible bonding web and anti-fraying solution if necessary, as before.

APPLIQUÉ BED LINEN

Customized bed linen is very simple to make and will give a real lift to bedroom decor. These designs can be added along borders or scattered across the main fabirc — it all depends upon how adventurous you feel. The duvet cover uses a variation on the technique of cut-work appliqué, meaning that the design is cut out from the main fabric and a contrasting colour stitched underneath.

1 Draw star shapes on to paper or thin card and cut out. Draw round the stars on to scraps of coloured fabric using a vanishing fabric marker, allowing a 1 cm (½ in) seam allowance.

2 Cut out the fabric stars, snipping into the seam allowance up to the drawn outline as shown. Do not cut into the actual star shape.

3 With wrong sides facing, iron the seam allowance back on to the star to make neat edges.

MATERIALS AND EQUIPMENT YOU WILL NEED

PENCIL • PAPER OR THIN CARD • PAPER SCISSORS • SCRAPS OF COTTON FABRIC • VANISHING FABRIC MARKER • DRESSMAKER'S SCISSORS
IRON • COTTON PILLOWCASE • DRESSMAKER'S PINS • NEEDLE • TACKING THREAD • SEWING MACHINE • CONTRASTING SEWING
THREADS • DUVET COVER • EMBROIDERY SCISSORS

4 Position the stars along one edge of the pillowcase, pin and tack in place.

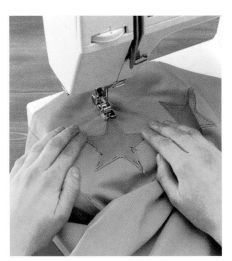

5 Using a contrasting colour, use a running stitch to machine-stitch the stars in place. Remove the tacking threads.

6 For the duvet cover, for each circular motif you will need to cut out two circles of fabric in contrasting colours.

7 Using the star template from the pillowcase, draw round the star on to the wrong side of one of the fabric circles.

8 Use sharp embroidery scissors to cut out the star 5 mm (¼ in) in from the outline, leaving the circle intact. Snip into the seam allowances as before and, wrong sides facing, iron the seam allowance to form a neat edge.

9 Place the circle with the cut-out motif on top of the right side of the remaining circle, pin and tack in place. ▶

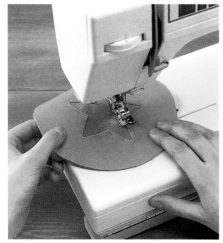

10 Machine-stitch round the edges of the star shapes and remove the tacking threads.

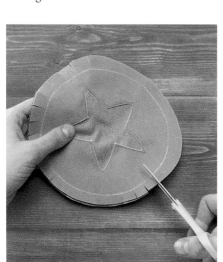

11 Snip round the circle, 1 cm (½ in) in from the edge, and press in place as before.

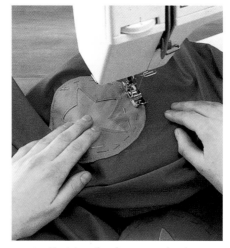

12 Position the shapes on the duvet cover, pin and tack in place. Machine-stitch round the circles using plain and decorative stitches in contrasting colours. Remove the tacking stitches.

ORGANZA EVENING BAG

THIS EXQUISITE LITTLE BAG IS DECORATED WITH DELICATE ORGANZA FLOWERS, SIMPLY MADE OF FRINGED AND GATHERED BIAS STRIPS. A SINGLE FLOWER IS STITCHED TO THE GOLD RIBBON TIES TO NEATEN THE ENDS. THE BAG IS TOO BEAUTIFUL TO HIDE AWAY IN A DRAWER WHEN NOT IN USE — FILL IT WITH POT POURRI OR HERBS AND HANG IT ON A DRESSING TABLE OR BEDPOST. A LARGER BAG COULD BE MADE TO HOLD A NIGHTDRESS.

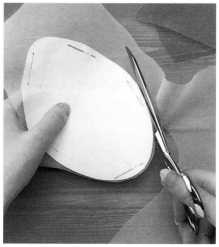

1 Draw an oval shape on paper, 14 cm (5½ in) long and 11 cm (4½ in) at the widest point. Cut out, pin on to cream organza and cut round. Cut two pieces of blue organza 18 cm (7½ in) wide and 20 cm (7¾ in) high.

2 Place the two pieces of blue organza together, fold in half and machine-stitch the short side. Right sides facing, tack to the cream organza oval then stitch. Turn the bag right side out.

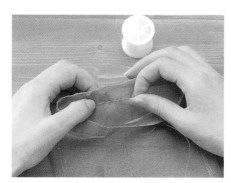

3 To make the ribbon casing, fold over 1 cm (½ in) on the open edge and slip-stitch. Use transparent thread for all the hand stitching.

4 Cut 11 different-coloured organza strips on the bias, varying the width between 1.5 cm (⅝ in) and 3 cm (1½ in). ▶

MATERIALS AND EQUIPMENT YOU WILL NEED
PAPER • PENCIL • TAPE MEASURE OR RULER • PAPER SCISSORS • DRESSMAKER'S PINS • CREAM ORGANZA • DRESSMAKER'S SCISSORS •
40 CM (16 IN) BLUE ORGANZA • SEWING MACHINE AND MATCHING THREADS • NEEDLE • TACKING THREAD • TRANSPARENT SEWING THREAD •
SCRAPS OF CONTRASTING ORGANZA • SAFETY PIN • 50 CM (20 IN) NARROW GOLD RIBBON

5 Fringe one side of each strip by pulling and rubbing the threads. Work a line of large running stitches along the other edge of each strip.

7 Stitch each flower at the base to secure the shape.

9 Stitch the double flowers on to the bag, arranging them in a bouquet.

6 Pull the end of the thread to gather the organza, at the same time twisting the strip around your finger to create a flower shape.

8 To make a fuller flower, place two flower shapes together, one inside another. Stitch together with small stitches at the base. Make another four flowers in the same way, mixing the colours. Leave one flower single.

10 Fasten a safety pin to the end of the ribbon and thread it through the casing. Knot the ends then stitch the single flower to the knot.

ANGELIC BABYGROW

This enchanting outfit is guaranteed to make any baby look sweet and good! Position the wings on the upper part of the babygrow, approximately where the baby's shoulder blades will lie. The wings are lightly padded with a layer of wadding to give a slightly quilted effect when you machine-stitch the outlines. The same technique and design could be used to decorate other baby clothes.

1 Trace the wing shapes from the back of the book and make templates (see Basic Techniques). Using a fabric marker, draw around the top wing shape on to a piece of interfacing then iron on to the reverse of the blue fabric. Iron interfacing on to the reverse of the pink fabric.

2 Draw around the bottom wing shape on to the interfacing side of the pink fabric. Cut out both shapes, leaving extra blue fabric on the edge marked "A", as shown. Repeat steps 1 and 2 for the other wing.

3 Tack the two parts of each wing together, making sure that the two pieces of interfacing butt together. ▶

MATERIALS AND EQUIPMENT YOU WILL NEED
TRACING PAPER • SOFT PENCIL • PAPER OR THIN CARD • PAPER SCISSORS • FADING FABRIC MARKER • LIGHTWEIGHT IRON-ON INTERFACING •
IRON • BLUE AND PINK JERSEY FABRIC • EMBROIDERY SCISSORS • NEEDLE • TACKING THREAD • LIGHTWEIGHT WADDING •
SEWING MACHINE AND MATCHING THREADS • BABYGROW

4 Tack each wing on to a piece of wadding.

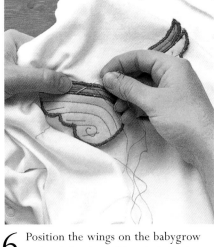

6 Position the wings on the babygrow and tack in place. Slip-stitch in place, using matching threads.

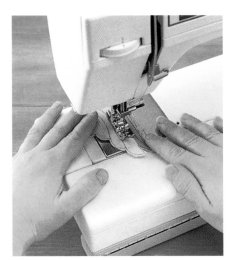

5 Using blue thread machine-stitch around the edges of the wings, using a straight stitch. Cut away the excess wadding. Machine-stitch the decorative outlines. Set the machine to satin stitch and stitch round the edges of the wing.

RIBBON CUSHION

COLLECT DIFFERENT WOVEN AND BROCADE RIBBONS FOR THIS PRETTY CUSHION THEN MACHINE-STITCH THEM ON TO A TICKING BACKGROUND, USING THE STRIPES A GUIDE. ALWAYS STITCH FROM THE TOP DOWN TO AVOID PUCKERING THE RIBBONS. COMPLETE THE PERIOD EFFECT WITH AN ELABORATE BRAID BORDER. IF YOU ONLY HAVE SHORT LENGTHS OF RIBBON AVAILABLE, MAKE A SMALL SLEEP PILLOW OR HERB BAG AND FILL IT WITH POT POURRI OR LAVENDER.

1 Cut the ribbons into 35 cm (14 in) lengths. Arrange them to make a pleasing design.

2 Starting from the righthand side, machine-stitch the wide ribbons on to the ticking background with a close zigzag stitch. Follow the stripes to keep the ribbons straight.

3 Add the narrow ribbons, stitching them on top of the previous layer.

4 Measure the finished size of 33 x 53 cm (13 x 21 in) and mark with a fabric marker. If necessary, trim the ribbons to this size.

5 Stitch a narrow double hem along one edge of each 33 cm (13 in) square of fabric for the back opening. Right sides facing, pin one side to each short edge of the ribbon appliqué so that the trimmed edges face inwards. Stitch all round, leaving a 1 cm (½ in) seam. Turn the cushion cover right side out.

6 Starting at one corner, stitch the braid all round the cushion, using slip stitch. Gather the braid slightly at the corners. Conceal the join in the ends at the final corner. Insert the cushion pad.

MATERIALS AND EQUIPMENT YOU WILL NEED

EMBROIDERY SCISSORS • APPROXIMATELY 1 M (1 YD) EACH OF TEN RIBBONS, IN DIFFERENT WIDTHS • TWO 36 x 46 CM (14 x 18 IN) TICKING, WITH THE STRIPES PARALLEL TO THE SHORT SIDES • SEWING MACHINE AND MATCHING THREADS • RULER • FADING FABRIC MARKER • TWO 33 CM (13 IN) SQUARES OF FABRIC, FOR THE BACK • 155 CM (61 IN) DECORATIVE BRAID • 30 x 40 CM (12 x 16 IN) CUSHION PAD

ROSE PETAL LAMPSHADE

ORGANZA WORKS PARTICULARLY WELL USED TO DECORATE A PLAIN LAMP-SHADE, WITH THE LIGHT INTENSIFYING THE DELICATE COLOURS. THE PETAL SHAPES ARE APPLIED IN LAYERS TO CREATE A THREE-DIMENSIONAL EFFECT. ADJUST THE NUMBER OF PETALS, DEPENDING ON THE SIZE OF THE SHADE. MIX TONING COLOURS — SAY, REDS AND PINKS OR PURPLES AND LILACS. USE A LOW WATTAGE BULB AND DO NOT LEAVE THE LAMP UNATTENDED.

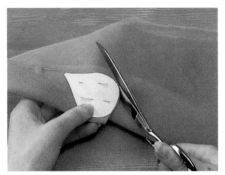

1 Draw two petal shapes on paper, one larger than the other. Using the large template, cut out approximately 20 petals in different shades of organza.

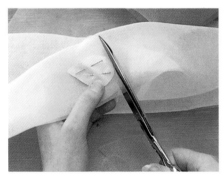

2 Cut out approximately 20 small petals, using the smaller template.

3 Using a paintbrush, glue a row of large petals 5 cm (2 in) above the bottom edge of the shade, alternating the colours. Apply the glue only at the pointed end of each petal. Overlap the petals as shown to cover the shade.

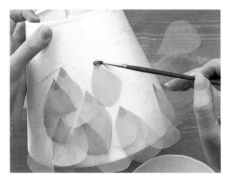

4 Gradually work up the shade to the top, mixing large and small petals and varying the colours. Leave to dry.

5 Alternatively, stitch each petal in place, using transparent thread. Try not to stitch through the whole shade but only into the silk or cotton surface.

6 Using a small amount of glue or a needle and transparent thread, fix the trimming round the top of the shade. Fold to the inside and glue or stitch in place.

MATERIALS AND EQUIPMENT YOU WILL NEED

PENCIL • PAPER • PAPER SCISSORS • DRESSMAKER'S PINS • 40 x 40 CM (16 x 16 IN) EACH OF THREE TONING SHADES OF SILK ORGANZA • DRESSMAKER'S SCISSORS • SMALL PAINTBRUSH • PVA GLUE • SAUCER • SILK OR COTTON LAMPSHADE • NEEDLE • TRANSPARENT SEWING THREAD • LAMPSHADE TRIMMING

LACE CUSHION

NATURAL LINEN FABRIC AND SCRAPS OF HEAVY WHITE LACE COMBINE BEAU-
TIFULLY IN THIS SMALL CUSHION, FINISHED WITH PEARL BEADS AND A
FRINGED EDGE. USE SEVERAL DIFFERENT STYLES OF GUIPURE LACE TO MAKE THE
DESIGN INTERESTING. THE SAME IDEA WOULD WORK EQUALLY WELL ON A DRESS-
ING GOWN OR DRAWSTRING BAG. TO PREVENT THE EDGES OF THE LACE MOTIFS
FROM FRAYING, PAINT ON AN ANTI-FRAYING SOLUTION.

1 Draw a large letter, about 12 cm
(4¾ in) high, on paper and cut out to
make a template. Draw round the
template on to the right side of one linen
square. Cut out lace motifs, choosing
shapes that will fit the shape of the letter.

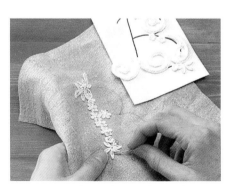

2 Treat the lace edges with anti-fraying
solution. Leave to dry. Transfer the
lace motifs to the linen and tack in place.

3 Using white sewing thread, stitch
the motifs in place with small stab
stitches. Wrong sides facing, hand- or
machine-stitch the two squares of linen
together, 3 cm (1½ in) from the edge,
leaving a 5cm (2 in) gap along one side.
Pull away threads for 2 cm (¾ in) to fringe
the edges. Fill with a small amount of
wadding. Slip-stitch the gap.

4 Stitch the narrow lace edging along
the stitch line, to cover the stitches
and decorate the edges.

5 Using a beading needle, stitch tiny
pearl beads to the centre of the
flower-shaped lace motifs. Stitch a daisy
motif to each corner of the cushion.

MATERIALS AND EQUIPMENT YOU WILL NEED
PENCIL • PAPER • PAPER SCISSORS • FADING FABRIC MARKER • TWO 22 CM (8½ IN) SQUARES OF HEAVYWEIGHT NATURAL-COLOURED LINEN •
EMBROIDERY SCISSORS • SCRAPS OF WHITE GUIPURE LACE, INCLUDING SCROLL AND FLOWER MOTIFS • ANTI-FRAYING SOLUTION • NEEDLE •
TACKING THREAD • SEWING MACHINE (OPTIONAL) • WHITE SEWING THREAD • WADDING • 90 CM (35½ IN) NARROW WHITE LACE EDGING •
BEADING NEEDLE • TINY PEARL BEADS

FELTED APPLIQUÉ ORGANZA

IN THIS BEAUTIFUL TRANSLUCENT PIECE THE DESIGN IS MADE USING WOOL FIBRES, WHICH ARE SANDWICHED BETWEEN LAYERS OF NET AND ORGANZA AND THEN FELTED TOGETHER. FELTING IS QUITE A MESSY PROCESS SO MAKE SURE YOU HAVE PLENTY OF SPACE TO WORK IN. USE AS A CURTAIN OR ROOM DIVIDER.

1 Cut the lengths of organza and net in half. Place one piece of organza on top of one piece of net.

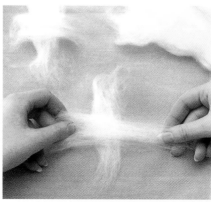

3 Place more layers of wool horizontally on top. Then place a third layer vertically on top. If desired, add silk fibre to the wool fibre.

4 Trim the edges of each mound of wool, shaping them into squares or rectangles.

2 Pull out a thin layer of wool fibre approximately 5 cm (2 in) long. Lay the wool vertically on the organza as shown. Repeat to make a design.

5 Repeat the vertical and horizontal layering process all around the edges of the organza, to create a woollen border, as shown.

MATERIALS AND EQUIPMENT YOU WILL NEED

DRESSMAKER'S SCISSORS • 3.2 M (3½ YD) WHITE SILK ORGANZA • 3.2 M (3½ YD) PLASTIC NET • 750 G (2 LB) WHITE MERINO WOOL FIBRE • 25 G (1 OZ) SILK FIBRE (OPTIONAL) • NEEDLE AND MATCHING THREAD • LARGE PLASTIC SHEET • WASHING-UP LIQUID • IRON

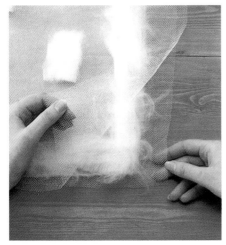

6 Place the other pieces of net on top of the design.

8 Protect the work surface with a sheet of plastic then wet the fabric "sandwich" with water.

10 Roll up the fabric along one edge. Start to felt it by rubbing the surface gently with your hands in a circular movement for a few minutes, then unroll the fabric.

7 Hand stitch the two pieces of net and organza together all around the edge with large stitches.

9 Apply washing-up liquid over the fabric, to help the felting process.

11 Continue rolling and felting each side for aproximately 15 minutes. Wash the fabric thoroughly with warm water, open out flat and leave to dry. ▶

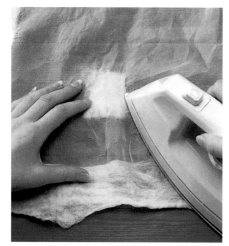

12 Remove the top layer of net and iron the felted fabric carefully.

14 The loops may be used to hang the fabric from a wooden frame to make a screen, or to hang from a window or corner of a room.

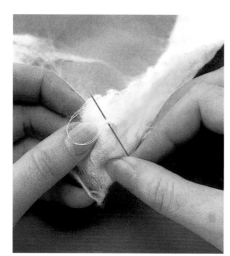

13 Stitch loops of thread on to each corner.

SEASIDE CHAIR

Transform a plain director's chair with a bold design of multi-coloured flags flying from yellow sandcastles. The repeat motifs are fused on to the removable chair back with iron-on bonding web then machine-stitched in place. Hand-embroidered French knots add an extra jaunty flourish. Work out how many sandcastles will fit on the chair back and space them evenly.

1 Iron the fusible bonding web on to the reverse side of the yellow fabric and the fabrics for the flags.

2 Trace the sandcastle and flag shapes from the back of the book on to paper or thin card to make templates and cut out (see Basic Techniques). Using a soft pencil, draw round the templates on to the bonding web. Cut out.

3 Remove the back from the chair. Peel off the backing paper from each shape and position on the right side of the chair back, as shown, with a flag above each sandcastle turret. Iron in place.

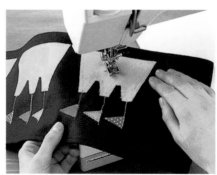

4 Machine-stitch round the edge of each shape with a close zigzag stitch. For the flagpoles, stitch a line of straight stitch to join the flags to the turrets.

5 Stitch a star on each sandcastle. Using embroidery thread, work a French knot at the top of each flag.

6 Cut a piece of fabric to cover the appliqué design, allowing an extra 5 mm (¼ in) seam. Turn under the seam and pin in place over the back of the appliqué, with wrong sides together. Slip-stitch in place.

MATERIALS AND EQUIPMENT YOU WILL NEED

IRON • IRON-ON FUSIBLE BONDING WEB • YELLOW FABRIC, FOR THE SANDCASTLES • SCRAPS OF DIFFERENT-COLOURED FABRICS, FOR THE FLAGS •
TRACING PAPER • SOFT PENCIL • PAPER OR THIN CARD • PAPER SCISSORS • DRESSMAKER'S SCISSORS • DIRECTOR'S CHAIR • IRON •
SEWING MACHINE AND MATCHING THREADS • NEEDLE • SOFT COTTON EMBROIDERY THREADS • CONTRASTING FABRIC, TO LINE THE CHAIR BACK •
DRESSMAKER'S PINS

TEMPLATES

ANGELIC BABYGROW PP 79–81

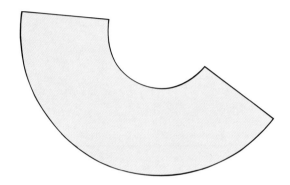

COUNTRY CANDLESHADES PP 48–49

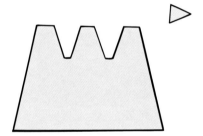

SEASIDE CHAIR PP 92–93

ALPHABET APRON PP 32–33

KITCHEN COLLAGE PP 28–31

TOY BAG PP 40–41

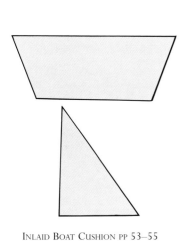

INLAID BOAT CUSHION PP 53–55

ANGEL STOCKING PP 37–39

HEARTS AND STARS BLANKET PP 42–45

SUPPLIERS & ACKNOWLEDGEMENTS

CONTRIBUTORS

The author and publishers would like to thank the following for their designs:

Victoria Brown
Christmas Tree Stars, Felt Curtain and Angelic Babygrow.

Lucinda Ganderton
Hands and Hearts Throw, Country Candleshades, Broderie Perse Tablecloth, Ribbon Cushion and Lace Cushion.

Jo Gordon
Heart-warming Hats.

Isabel Stanley
Mosaic Velvet Cushion.

Daniella Zimmerman Organza Evening Bag, Rose Petal Lampshade and Felted Appliqué Organza.

SUPPLIERS

United Kingdom

John Lewis
(consult your telephone directory for your nearest branch)
Wide range of sewing equipment and materials, fabrics and sewing machines

Silken Strands
33 Links Way
Gatelly, Cheedle
Cheshire, SK8 4LA
Machine embroidery threads, available mail order

Canada

Dressew
337 W Hastings Street
Vancouver, BC
682 6196
Sewing and craft materials

Australia

Lincraft
(stores in every capital city except Darwin)
For store addresses telephone (03) 9875 7575

INDEX

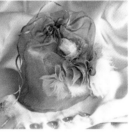